21 DAYS
——— to a ———
DEEPER LIFE

An interactive devotional
with excerpts from
THE DEEPER LIFE
Satisfying the 8 Vital Longings of Your Soul

DANIEL HENDERSON
with Brenda Brown

STRATEGIC RENEWAL

© 2019 by Daniel Henderson

Published by Strategic Renewal

www.strategicrenewal.com

Printed in the United States of America

All rights reserved. No part of this publication may be reproduced, stored in a retrieval system, or transmitted in any form or by any means—for example, electronic, photocopy, recording—without the prior written permission of the publisher. The only exception is brief quotations in printed reviews.

ISBN 9781734197310

Emphasis in Scripture shown by italics is the author's.

Unless otherwise indicated, Scripture quotations are from the New King James Version. Copyright © 1982 by Thomas Nelson, Inc. Used by permission. All rights reserved.

Scripture quotations identified NASB are from the New American Standard Bible®, copyright © 1960, 1962, 1963, 1968, 1971, 1973, 1975, 1977, 1995 by The Lockman Foundation. Used by permission.

Scripture quotations identified ESV are from The Holy Bible, English Standard Version ® (ESV®), copyright © 2001 by Crossway, a publishing ministry of Good news Publishers. Used by permission. All rights reserved. ESV Text Edition: 2007.

Scripture quotations identified AMP are from the Amplified® Bible, copyright © 1954, 1958, 1962, 1964, 1965, 1987 by The Lockman Foundation. Used by permission.

In the Old Testament, when it came to spiritual renewal, God always had a man in mind to lead the way. Having sat under the leadership of Daniel Henderson, it may well be he is God's leader for our generation, helping to set the stage for true spiritual renewal in the church today!"

–Joni Eareckson Tada, Joni and Friends International Disability Center

"As a pastor for over two decades, Daniel Henderson was passionate about helping churches experience authentic renewal. Today, as a pastor to pastors, Daniel inspires leaders to renewed courage and impact. Now, he writes once again to help you with a unique and practical plan for spiritual authenticity. In a world of constant distraction and chronic discouragement, this book offers strategic focus and hope for the daily journey."

–Mark Batterson, New York Times bestselling author of The Circle Maker

"Daniel Henderson has his finger on the pulse of Christians who are saved and growing spiritually but who are missing the connections between their theology and an actual life of joy and purpose…. Without being programmatic or too tactical, Henderson provides a sound process for people to live the life God originally intended them to live."

–Jeff Spadafora, director of global coaching services for Halftime

"Daniel's ministry is extremely refreshing as he communicates in a down-to-earth way about the questions and issues that we all face in our Christian walk. He makes it plain – equipping readers with practical how-tos for transforming their spiritual journeys."

–Chrissy Cymbala Toledo, worship leader, The Chicago Tabernacle

"Daniel Henderson has not only been a mentor to me, I've watched him invest in thousands of young leaders. His commitment to fostering spiritual renewal in the church is fueling the faith of generations."

–Johnnie Moore, President, The KAIROS Company

Contents

Foreword by Jim Cymbala 7

Introduction 9

Day 1. The Power of Daily Renewal 15

THEOLOGY

Day 2. Who is God? *Part 1* 17

Day 3. Who is God? *Part 2* 21

Day 4 Who is God? *Part 3* 23

IDENTITY

Day 5. Who am I? *Part 1* 29

Day 6. Who am I? *Part 2* 33

Day 7. Who am I? *Part 3* 37

PURPOSE

Day 8. Why am I Here? *Part 1* 41

Day 9. Why am I Here? *Part 2* 45

Day 10. Why am I Here? *Part 3* 49

VALUES

Day 11. What Really Matters? *Part 1* 53

Day 12. What Really Matters? *Part 2* 57

PRIORITIES

Day 13. What Shall I Do? *Part 1* 61

Day 14. What Shall I Do? *Part 2* 65

GOALS

Day 15. How Shall I Do It? *Part 1* 69

Day 16. How Shall I Do It? *Part 2* 73

TIME

Day 17. When Shall I Do It? *Part 1* 77

Day 18. When Shall I Do It? *Part 2* 81

LEGACY

Day 19. How Will I Finish? *Part 1* 85

Day 20. How Will I Finish? *Part 2* 89

CONCLUSION

Day 21. The Journey Begins 93

About the Authors 96

Foreword

In *The Deeper Life: Satisfying the 8 Vital Longings of Your Soul*, Daniel Henderson helps believers from every walk of life experience renewal by making specific application of the gospel to daily life. The gospel of Jesus Christ brings us into an accurate and vital understanding of the one true God. It transforms how we see ourselves in this world. It ignites meaningful purpose and guides the way we manage our daily priorities and decisions.

This study shows us this reality, in the most practical of terms. We all want to come to the end of this life with the assurance that we have deposited a legacy of spiritual authenticity and eternal significance in the hearts of those who have known us well. I pray you will embrace this message and engage in this clear path of living a more intentional and fruitful life for the glory of our Lord Jesus Christ.

Pastor Jim Cymbala
The Brooklyn Tabernacle Church

Introduction

"Men for the sake of getting a living forget to live."
Margaret Fuller

The Musée Rodin in Paris, France is dedicated to the works of the French sculptor Auguste Rodin. Probably most famous of all Rodin's creations is the original work titled, *The Thinker*. First cast in 1902, this bronze figure of a nude man sits atop a marble pedestal. Hand on his chin, looking down but thinking deep, he ponders. And we wonder. What is he thinking about? My first thought is that he must be working hard to remember where he left his clothes. In reality, he simply represents the journey of all human earth travelers. As the biblical writer Job noted, we came into the world naked, and naked we will return. Stripped of all the superficial trappings of life, we are left with our thoughts and looking for answers.

The truth is, we were created to think deeply about something more than meets the eye in this life. The Bible says God has placed "eternity in our hearts," compelling us to yearn for conclusions that will satisfy the soul. We were made to ask questions; to discover meaning beyond mere physical existence. Thus begins the quest.

We all yearn for a compelling mission in life, if only we could figure out what it is supposed to be. We feel the need to be guided by a clear set of values and long to leave a lasting legacy, but lose our way in the fog of daily distractions. The demands of work, family, church, and home leave us feeling overwhelmed. Each night our "to do" lists remain full of undone tasks. As we doze off to sleep, we feel this haunting sense that we will never get on top of things. When the alarm goes off the next morning, we quickly shower, eat, and rush out the door, saying to ourselves, *I've got to get going.* Perhaps we would do well to ask, *Where am I going?* and *Why am I in such a hurry to get there?* followed by *How's this working for me?*

In the busyness of adapting to daily demands and the orders of a noisy world, we've forgotten to consider that God has a plan for us to win the daily battle against shallow living. He wants us to sink roots deep into the soil of his promises as we allow His truth to absorb into the core of our soul.

Eight Questions and the Answers That Shape Your Legacy

This book will guide you to recognize and address the deepest needs and questions of the soul. As you consider the biblical answers, you'll be able to create specific, practical affirmations for daily review.

- **The Question:** Who is God?
- **The Issue:** My theology

- **The Question**: Who am I?
- **The Issue:** My identity

- **The Question:** Why am I here?
- **The Issue:** My purpose

- **The Question:** What really matters?
- **The Issue:** My values

- **The Question:** What shall I do?
- **The Issue:** My priorities

- **The Question:** How shall I do it?
- **The Issue:** My goals

- **The Question:** When shall I do it?
- **The Issue:** My time

- **The Question:** How will I finish?
- **The Issue:** My legacy

In summary, you will discover that your theology is the basis of your identity. Your identity is expressed through a clear purpose. Your purpose is guided by values. Your values determine your priorities. Your priorities are implemented by your goals. Your goals are accomplished by your stewardship of time. All of this, when understood clearly and embraced daily, results in a legacy that really matters.

Pearls of Daily Wisdom

In a recent leadership conference, I heard Jim Collins, professor and author of books like *Built to Last* and *Good to Great*, describe his goal as a teacher. He said his job is to offer thought-provoking ideas and to leave people with "grains of sand in their minds." These ideas create such an irritation that over time, through great thought and contemplation, they become pearls of wisdom.

This book is designed to leave grains of truth in your mind. The questions are designed to be delightfully provoking. And while the answers aren't always easily arrived at, they are clearly worth the energy. Serious consideration of them will invariably form pearls of discovery that will result in your life being more integrated than ever before. The effort and valuable time invested will prove profitable—both for now and eternity.

Ultimately we want God to reveal to our hearts the truth of who He is and then show us how to live. This book will help you clarify and write out these essential truths. The approach has worked for us and helped thousands of others. It can work for you. Please join us on this twenty-one-day journey to a deeper life.

Daniel Henderson
–with Brenda Brown

Join the Interactive 21 Days to a Deeper Life Experience!

To help you in this deeper life journey, go online to access a daily playlist of prayers to be used alongside this book. Here's how it works:

- Read the *Deeper Life* devotional for that day.
- Go online to www.strategicrenewal.com/21days to join us in the corresponding prayer for that day.
- Pray and ask the Lord to reveal His answers to the deep longings in your soul.
- Write down your answers to each question in words that express the needs and journey of your own life. Trust the Holy Spirit to give you insight and clarity.
- Begin a daily habit of renewing your mind and heart through the answers you discover through this process.
- If you desire to go even deeper in this journey, go to strategicrenewal.com to order The Deeper Life book or small group DVD series. To realize the full potential of this renewal experience, you can sign-up for personal or small group coaching at strategicrenewal.com.

DAY 1

The Power of Daily Renewal

> The hardest thing about the Christian life
> is that it is so *daily*.
>
> –*Daniel Henderson*

The apostle Paul was the classic first-century example of a man climbing the ladder of success, only to find that it was leaning against the wrong wall. Everyone in his day knew him as Saul. His eventual name change reflected a true transformation of identity. It all started with an encounter with the living Christ, sparking some agonizing questions, resulting in a pursuit of the right answers, manifested in a life of renewal and legacy of incredible significance.

Saul was a driven man, passionate to get to the top and make a name for himself. On this day the Jewish zealot was on the road again. He headed north from Jerusalem, hot on the trail of those Christians who had fled his persecuting passion. Saul could not tolerate these people of the Way who posed a threat to his tightly organized world.

But it all changed in a flash—literally. An inexplicable bright light at mid-day left him on his face, blind and baffled. In that hour of crisis, he was confronted with the truth about what was wrong with his life and how he needed to change his ways. In the days that followed, he would contemplate answers to the most important questions he had ever asked.

They spilled out in that defining moment as He encountered the living Jesus. He asked, "Who are you, Lord?" And as naturally as *A* follows *B*, he also inquired, "What do you want me to do?" (Acts 9:5-6 NKJV).

The answers he discovered made all the difference in the world—his world and ours. Today, the reality of Saul's quest is very much like ours. We need an encounter with the living Christ. We need to ask Him for the answers to the questions deep in the soul. Ultimately, we want Him to reveal to our hearts the truth of who He is and show us how to live. Then, we can renew our minds in these conclusions and clarifications in order to weave them into the very fabric of our thoughts and lifestyle.

I have concluded from my own spiritual quest, as well as from shepherding thousands of souls in pastoral ministry, that the hardest thing about the Christian life is that it is so DAILY. The rising sun on our every day journey brings the opportunity to win or lose in the spiritual contest. The glowing dusk calls out to us to evaluate the real meaning of the day and the eternal value of our efforts.

That is why this book was written. You are holding in your hand a guide for your daily "win." It is a win that matters and a victory that is biblical. The process is proven. But, like anything of value, you will have to work for it. Dig in, because the effort will be well worth it. I pray it will help you live a deeper life by providing a plan for transformation and triumph—daily.

> Go deeper by joining us in prayer for Day 1.
> Visit www.strategicrenewal.com/21days

DAY 2

Who is God?

> The most important thing about a person
> is what comes to mind when they think about God.
>
> –A. W. Tozer

If you were even remotely tuned into television during the mid to late 1990s, you are familiar with America's love affair with Gidget the dog. She became so popular that she flew first-class, opened up the New York Stock Exchange and even made an appearance at Madison Square Garden. You will remember her as the Taco Bell Chihuahua, probably assuming it was a boy dog. Many of her lines became mainstream to American culture. "¡Yo quiero Taco Bell!" "Viva Gorditas!," "Drop the chalupa!"

My personal favorite first appeared in 1998. The scene featured the downtown streets of a large city late at night. Homemade signs were posted in various places pointing the way to a plate of tacos on the sidewalk. Gidget stood expectantly near her "bait." In her mouth was a rope tied to a stick holding up a box. She was ready for her unsuspecting prey. In the darkness of the night she called out, "Here, Lizard, Lizard."

Unexpectedly, an imposing shadow steals the moment. A hungry and aggressive Godzilla appears. The little dog promptly drops the rope and in apparent shock utters, "Uh-oh! I think I need a bigger box!"

Like the little canine, we are all on a quest to find something that ultimately proves bigger than our expectation or capacity. We need the bigger and better box of a clear biblical understanding and a regular renewal in the truth of the one true God.

Have you ever considered that all of your life is ultimately an expression of your theology? The word *theology* comes from two Greek terms, "theos" which means "God" and "logos" which primarily refers to the "study of" something. For our purposes, we'll refer to it simply as "our view of God."

Proverbs 9:10 and Psalm 111:10 tell us that "the fear of the Lord is the beginning of wisdom." Applying practical truth to daily life begins with our understanding of God. Knowing how we should live is anchored in the bedrock of our God concept.

An Essential Foundation

The first home my wife and I purchased was in the Seattle area. It was a new house. We were the first buyers in the neighborhood so we selected our lot, floor plan, and preferences for the various amenities. Once construction began we drove by our "home-to-be" virtually every day. It seemed like they took forever in digging the trenches and pouring a complete and solid foundation. Many weeks later as we watched the walls, roof, exterior, and interior eventually being completed we understood why the foundation was so essential. A careless and incomplete foundation would have been the demise of the entire home. All of the fine carpentry, new windows, colorful carpet, and fresh paint would have ultimately been for no purpose if the house crumbled on the moorings of a lousy foundation.

In life, we can often be in such a hurry to create a strategic plan, build a career and establish a family that we inadvertently ignore the bedrock issue of a defined and applied theology. If we want a life that stands through the storms, it is essential to be grounded in this solid truth.

Life, Breath, and All Things

The apostle Paul addressed the spiritually curious of his day. "Men of Athens, I perceive that in all things you are very religious; for as I was passing through and considering the objects of your worship, I even found an altar with this inscription: "TO THE UNKNOWN GOD." (Acts 17:23–24) Not long ago, I stood in the very area called Mars Hill where Paul made these keen observations about the culture of his day. The majesty of the Acropolis and the beauty of the Parthenon have certainly lost their luster and influence since Paul stood in their shadow exchanging ideas with the philosophers of his day. Yet, the cultural landscape of irreligious modern-day Greece still speaks of mankind's failed quest to discover a life-changing understanding of the one true God.

Standing among the crowds, Paul explained that all of man's attempts to find God through idols, man-made systems and the religious trappings of buildings and icons reflect a wrong understanding of the one true God.

We cannot erect a building high enough or a bridge far enough to reach God. Our efforts will crumble every time. He is the creator, and He is working all around us to move us to find in Him real life and meaning. Now, he is calling us to turn from our self-seeking and sin to His son, Jesus Christ. This Christ has risen from the dead, proving his deity and validating the truth of His message. He is the one that will one day judge the world. Hear his call to your heart today.

Go deeper by joining us in prayer for Day 2.
Visit www.strategicrenewal.com/21days

DAY 3

> God is.
>
> God is near.
>
> God is love,
>
> Longing to communicate himself to me.
>
> God the Almighty One
>
> Who worketh all in all,
>
> Is even now waiting to work in me,
>
> And make himself known.
>
> –*Andrew Murray*

The compelling distinction of biblical Christianity is not that we must search for God by our own merits. Rather, He created us, loves us, is working in us to seek Him, and is ready by the merits of Jesus Christ to bring us into a true understanding of Himself through a transforming relationship. A.W. Tozer says it this way, "God and man exist for each other and neither is satisfied without the other."[1]

In the Bible, God reveals Himself to call us to a compelling and accurate understanding of His character. He describes Himself in a variety of terms that help us to seek, know and experience Him. In His loving determination, God went even further than all of the biblical descriptions of truth in His written revelation. He so wants us to know Him that He entered our world to be seen, heard and

---

[1] A.W. Tozer, The Pursuit of God (Camp Hill, PA: Christian Publications, 2002), 2.

touched. His feet trod the streets of Jerusalem. Drops of His blood fell on the soil at Calvary.

The Gospel of John explains in chapter one (vv. 14-18), that we have seen His glory, "glory as of the only begotten from the Father… who is in the bosom of the Father, He has declared Him." Jesus is God's explanation of Himself. So, if you want to have a firm foundation of truth upon which to base your life, study Jesus Christ.

Beyond creation, Scripture, and the incarnate Word, believers are empowered for spiritual intimacy by the indwelling truth of the Spirit of God. If I wanted my children to really understand some truths in life, I would likely do three things: try to explain these truths, endeavor to demonstrate them, and even hire a personal tutor to assure that they are learning these realities. God, in His perfection, has provided a personal indwelling tutor. The Holy Spirit is the very presence of God, illumining our minds and guiding our hearts to a transformational understanding and application of who He is.

This happens only as you commit yourself to the Lordship of Jesus Christ as revealed in the written truth of God. Unless God indwells you, the basis for life decisions will forever be an insufficient support of facts and ideas. It will never be an integrated, firm foundation of truth.

God wants you to know Him even more than you want to know Him. When you make that commitment, by His resident power, knowledge, and wisdom, He will teach you about Himself. As you spend time with Him and study about Him, you will grow in your love and understanding of Him. This is how to develop the firm foundation of truth for your life.

> Go deeper by joining us in prayer for Day 3.
> Visit www.strategicrenewal.com/21days

DAY 4

> Taste and see that the Lord is good.
> Oh the joys of those who trust in Him!
>
> *Psalm 34:8*

Many of us might find ourselves living like practical atheists – our belief in God doesn't really change our lives. I believe that nothing is dynamic until it is specific. That's why it's good practice to write down your view of God. Author William Faulkner said, "I never know what I think about something until I've read what I've written on it."

So how do we take the ocean of biblical truth about God and distill it down to our thimble of understanding? Among all the attributes and names of God, which should you focus on for the sake of daily renewal? The following exercises will help you write out your personal theology statement in answer to the question "Who is God?"

Theology Discovery: My Struggles – His Character

Review the list of common personal struggles. Rank each one from 1 to 5, with 1 being never and 5 being frequent.

24 *21 Days to a Deeper Life*

____ Addictions	____ Greed
____ Anxiety	____ Insecurity
____ Anger	____ Isolation
____ Apathy	____ Laziness
____ Bitterness	____ Loneliness
____ Broken relationships	____ Lust/sensuality
____ Controlling	____ Materialism
____ Coveting	____ Moodiness
____ Craving comfort	____ Negativity
____ Critical	____ Pride
____ Depression	____ Selfishness
____ Dishonesty	____ Self-doubt
____ Discontent	____ Self-promotion
____ Discouragement	____ Starved for attention
____ Doubt	____ Uncertainty
____ Fear	____ Unkindness
____ Gluttony	____ Unloving

Now, identify four or five of those that ranked the highest. Using the list below, select one of the attributes of God associated with that struggle that you feel would best spark daily renewal. This will allow you to experience a daily renewal in the truth of God's character in order to overcome common personal struggles.

Addictions — Omnipotent, Gracious, Holy

Anxiety — Sovereign, Omniscient, Wise, Good

Anger — Long-Suffering, Sovereign, Merciful, Forgiving

Apathy — Holy, Faithful, Long-Suffering, Loving

Bitterness — Forgiving, Gracious, Merciful, Kind, Long-suffering

Broken relationships — Forgiving, Gracious, Merciful, Long-Suffering

Controlling — Sovereign, Trustworthy, Peace

Coveting — All-sufficient, Good, Just, Provider

Craving comfort — Good, Omniscient, Portion

Critical — Gracious, Forgiving, Merciful, Loving

Depression — Joy, All-Sufficient, Faithful

Dishonesty — Truth, Immutable, Holy, Righteous

Discontent — Good, All-sufficient, Wise

Discouragement — Faithful, Omniscient, Incomprehensible, Good

Doubt — Truth, Omniscient, Immutable, Wise

Fear — Sovereign, Good, Omniscient, Omnipotent, Omnipresent

Gluttony — Self-control, Omnipotent

Greed — Sovereign, Good, Righteous

Insecurity — Good, Faithful, Loving, Omnipotent

Isolation — Sovereign, Omnipresent, Triune

Laziness — Omniscient, Omnipotent

Loneliness — Omnipresent, Loving, Faithful

Lust/sensuality — Holy, Omniscient, Righteous, Omnipotent

Materialism — Eternal, Good, Faithful

Moodiness — Good, Long-Suffering, Immutable

Negativity — Good, Immutable, Sovereign

Pride — Sovereign, Holy, Omnipotent, Infinite

Selfishness — Righteous, Loving, Gracious, Merciful

Self-doubt — Truthful, Wise, Omnipotent

Self-promotion — Holy, Sovereign

Starved for attention — Omnipresent, Omniscient, Loving

Stressed/overwhelmed — Gracious, Just, Long-Suffering, Omnipotent, Omnipresent

Uncertainty — Sovereign, Righteous, Good, Omniscient, Immutable, Incomprehensible

Unkindness — Long-Suffering, Merciful, Gracious, Loving, Good

Unloving — Loving, Long-Suffering, Gracious, Good

Applying My Personal Theology

Reflecting on your answers, select the names or attributes of God that seem especially relevant to your unique challenges and individual journey. Use the following page to describe the difference this will make in your daily life as you begin to craft a personal Theology Statement.

The most important life question is not about a career, where to live, how big the paycheck is, or even about health. The most important question is "Who is God?"

Example:

My God is **Sovereign**

Therefore ***I do not have to be anxious because I know He is in control and has a perfect plan for my life.***

My God is …
Therefore …

My God is …
Therefore …

My God is …
Therefore …

My God is …
Therefore …

Go deeper by joining us in prayer for Day 4.
Visit www.strategicrenewal.com/21days

DAY 5

Who Am I?

*A healthy self-image is
seeing yourself as God sees you.
No more. No less.*

The first public appearance in Jesus' formal ministry included a powerful pronouncement about His identity. As he came out of the water at His baptism, the Father declared from heaven, "This is my beloved Son in whom I am well pleased." (Matthew 3:17).

Immediately following this paramount moment, Jesus was led into the wilderness for a season of preparation through fasting and prayer. At the end of this 40-day experience, Satan launched a direct attack, querying twice, "If you are the Son of God …" (Matthew 4:1-11). At the core of Jesus' ministry was the truth of His heaven-affirmed uniqueness. At the heart of Satan's attack against Him was an attempt to question His true identity. The same is true with every follower of Christ.

Early Identity Crises

My first recollection of an identity crisis dates back to my childhood reading of the book titled, *Are You My Mother?* In this story, a baby bird hatched while its mother is away and then wanders around his immediate world, asking, "Are you my mother?" He questions a dog, a swan, a heavy machinery crane, a bulldozer, and anything else in his path. Each answer fails to provide the helpful information needed in his search for self-identity. Happily, at the conclusion of the tale, he does find his mother and the story ends well.

Wandering and Wondering

In some sense we all can understand the crisis of this little bird. Even though we have learned to ask in a more sophisticated manner, we still wonder: "Am I significant?" "Where do I belong?" and "Who am I?" It seems that we all spend our lives either searching for, attempting to prove, or confidently expressing our identity.

The Basis of Your Identity

Wise Christians base their identity on the reliable foundation of biblical truth about God and what He says to be true. This becomes the key to a proper self-image. Our new and eternal life in Christ is the core of our true identity. Then, as we consistently renew our minds in His declarations of who we are, we can weather the skewed input of the world, our unreliable emotions, and the trials of this life with confidence.

Our Eternal Identity

Man is a spiritual creature by God's design. In Genesis 1:27 the Bible specifically and distinctively describes this: "God created man in His own image, in the image of God He created him; male and female He created them." God breathed life's breath into man, and man became a living soul. (Genesis 2:7) From the beginning of time, we have been spiritual beings, distinctively formed apart from trees, animals, plants, or any other expression of God's creation.

Man is created with a spiritual capacity. Eternity is in our hearts. Deep within we are aware of realities beyond this physical life. We have a God-given yearning for something more.

Spiritual on Purpose

As image bearers of God's life, we have been created for a purpose.

Just as He chose us in Him before the foundation of the world, that we should be holy and blameless before Him. In love He predestined us to adoption as sons through Jesus Christ to Himself, according to the kind intention of His will to the praise of the glory of His grace, which He freely bestowed on us in the Beloved.

Ephesians 1:4-6 NASB

This potential allows us to interact meaningfully with God and with each other. Being able to relate beyond the physical realm will be with us for eternity, as each person is an eternal soul.

Go deeper by joining us in prayer for Day 5.
Visit www.strategicrenewal.com/21days

DAY 6

> I always wanted to be somebody.
> Now I realize I should have been more specific.
>
> – *Lily Tomlin*

I'll never forget the night I sat in a Seattle hotel enjoying a few moments of personal conversation with Bill Bright, founder of Campus Crusade for Christ. After a special event where we shared the platform, I asked his advice about some ministry struggles I was encountering. Among many other words of wisdom, he made this statement: "Every soul is precious, but not every Christian is strategic."

It is one thing to know how precious I am to God as a valued and loved child. It is another thing to be submitted to Him so that His power might turn my new person into a life of supernatural impact.

Our effective identity is all about who we are in the light of the design and enabling of God's grace. Great insight on this is found in Ephesians 2:10 where we read that we are His workmanship. You may remember that the Greek word here is *poiema*. Literally, we are His poem—His tapestry, His masterpiece. Each of us is specifically designed to make a difference in this world as an expression of our new life. My friend Mark Batterson says, "You are unlike anyone who has ever lived. But that uniqueness isn't a virtue. It's a responsibility. Uniqueness is God's gift to you, and uniqueness is your gift to God. You owe it to yourself to be yourself. But more important, you owe it to the One who designed you and destined you."[2] We are stewards of our unique, effective identity.

Discovering Your Spiritual DNA

To understand the factors of our unique usefulness, I use the acronym: S-DNA, which stands for our spiritual DNA. Just as we all have an exact physical code (DNA), so God has made every Christian unique in how they are wired for impact and service. The "S-DNA" represents spiritual gifts, desires of the heart, natural talents, and aptitudes. Seen as a whole, these form a distinct and effective identity.[3]

First, we need to understand and utilize our *spiritual gifts*. The Bible says, "Now there are a variety of gifts . . . to each one is given the manifestation of the Spirit for the common good" (1 Corinthians 12:4, 7).

God has given each believer unique gifts that enable us to minister with supernatural ability and impact for the glory of God. The fullness of effective identity is not possible until our spiritual giftedness is understood.

We also have unique *desires of the heart* that express our God-given interests. "It is God who works in you both to *will* and to do for His good pleasure" (Philippians 2:13). God works through our desires to direct and motivate us in His purposes. We each have a unique heart, and that's part of God's design for effectiveness in our identity for Him.

Through *natural talents*, we are empowered by God for effec-

---

[2] Mark Batterson, *Soulprint* (Portland, OR: Multnomah, 2011), p. 2.
[3] I am indebted to Pastor Rick Warren for clarifying many of these concepts through his SHAPE acrostic.

tiveness in His service. Exodus 36:1 illustrates this: "Every skillful person in whom the Lord has put skill and understanding to know how to perform all the work in the construction of the sanctuary, shall perform in accordance with all that the Lord has commanded." Our specific natural abilities are part of our effective identity.

Aptitude is an expression of our individual personality, work style and approach to life. This uniqueness within each person is a vehicle for God. As Paul wrote in 1 Corinthians 12:6, "There are varieties of effects, but the same God who works all things in all persons."

Differences in aptitude can easily be seen in group dynamics. In an office, some workers are most productive in an organized environment where everything is in place. Others are comfortable with a little creative confusion. One person likes routine, another seeks variety. The same is true for families. Each household is made up of people with unique personalities. The best functioning families are those where parents respond to the differences in their children in a way that encourages development according to each individual aptitude. We all approach life in a variety of ways, yet God brings effectiveness out of our differences.

Lasting Integrity

A deeper, thoughtful, intentional life flows from understanding who God is, then understanding who you are in Christ. A confident expression of one's identity is found in knowing—a secure knowing, that is based on truth. This is the only sure foundation for a life of lasting integrity.

Go deeper by joining us in prayer for Day 6.
Visit www.strategicrenewal.com/21days

DAY 7

Who I am in Christ

In light of your life's journey, review the truths of what God says to be true about you. Circle those that counter the negative experiences or affirm the positive experiences.

I AM ACCEPTED IN CHRIST

John 1:2	I am God's child
John 15:15	I am Christ's friend
Romans 5:1	I have been justified
1 Cor. 6:17	I am united with the Lord and one with Him in spirit
1 Cor. 6:20	I have been bought with a price; I belong to God
1 Cor. 12:27	I am a member of Christ's Body
Ephesians 1:1	I am a saint
Ephesians 1:5	I have been adopted as God's child
Ephesians 2:18	I have direct access to God through the Holy Spirit
Colossians 1:14	I have been redeemed and forgiven of all my sins
Colossians 2:10	I am complete in Christ

I AM SECURE IN CHRIST

Romans 8:1, 2	I am free forever from condemnation
Romans 8:28	I am assured that all things work together for good
Romans 8:33, 34	I am free from any condemning charges against me
Romans 8:35	I cannot be separated from the love of God
2 Cor. 1:21	I have been established, anointed, and sealed by God
Colossians 3:3	I am hidden with Christ in God
Philippians 1:6	I am sure that the good work God has begun in me will be perfected
Philippians 3:20	I am a citizen of heaven
2 Timothy 1:7	I have been given a spirit of power, love and a sound mind
Hebrews 4:16	I can find grace and mercy in time of need
1 John 5:18	I am born of God and the evil one cannot touch me

I AM SIGNIFICANT IN CHRIST

Matthew 5:13, 14	I am the salt and light of the earth
John 15:15	I am a branch of the true vine, a channel of His life
John 15:16	I have been chosen and appointed to bear fruit
Acts 1:8	I am a personal witness of Christ
1 Cor. 3:16	I am God's temple

Who am I? Part 3 **39**

2 Cor. 5:17-20	I am a minister of reconciliation
2 Cor. 6:1	I am God's co-worker
Ephesians 2:6	I am seated with Christ in the heavenly realm
Ephesians 2:10	I am God's workmanship
Ephesians 3:12	I may approach God with freedom and confidence
Philippians 4:13	I can do all things through Christ who strengthens me

(Taken from "Living Free in Christ" by Neil Anderson 1993, Regal Books)

With these key truths in mind, now make an attempt to write a basic statement about your essential identity including any applications you feel are helpful. Don't worry about perfecting this statement; just let this be a starting point.

Example:

I, Daniel D. Henderson, am a new creature in Jesus Christ – a completely loved, fully accepted, and totally empowered child of the most loving, most high, most holy God. I have been created by His amazing grace for a life full of good works and God's glory though Christ my Lord.

Go deeper by joining us in prayer for Day 7.
Visit www.strategicrenewal.com/21days

DAY 8

Why am I Here?

*The great tragedy in life is not death,
but life without reason.*

Miles Monroe

David, after he had served the purpose of God in his own
generation, fell asleep and was laid among his fathers.

Acts 13:36

In the 2011 movie "Hugo," an orphaned boy is desperate to repair a broken machine called an automaton. Convinced that it held a secret message from his father, Hugo struggled to repair the machine in the hope of finding a purpose for his life. Disappointed by his inability to fix the contraption, 12 year old Hugo observed, "Maybe that's why a broken machine always makes me a little sad, because it isn't able to do what it was meant to do…. Maybe it's the same with people. If you lost your purpose, it's like you're broken."[4]

It's apparent in our world today that many people are broken. They have no idea why they are here. Until we understand our purpose, life really has no meaning. The fact is that God wants you to live a life of significance, a life that is clearly yours because of Him.

---

4   Quoted in *Hugo,* (Paramount Pictures, 2011).

Young Hugo later explained his philosophy regarding a purposeful life. "Machines never come with any extra parts, you know. They always come with the exact amount they need. So I figured if the entire world was one big machine, I couldn't be an extra part. I had to be here for some reason."[5]

We are all on this earth for a reason. The Amplified Bible describes this as a "a divinely implanted sense of a purpose working through the ages which nothing under the sun but God alone can satisfy" (Ecclesiastes 3:11). Proverbs 16:4 explains, "The Lord has made everything for its purpose, even the wicked for the day of trouble." (ESV)

God offers you an opportunity to live a life that, when it is over, you can look back and know that you lived well. I've heard it said many times that "You're not really ready to live until you know what you want written on your tombstone." If you were to die today, would those who know you be able to say, "This is why he or she lived." Is it clear to you why you are here? When this life comes to an end, will you look back and conclude that you have lived well and significantly?

Finding Joy

Helen Keller said, "Many persons have the wrong idea of what constitutes true happiness. It is not obtained through self-gratification, but through fidelity to a worthy purpose." A worthy purpose brings joy.

Jesus knew that. In Hebrews 12 we are told to fix our eyes on Jesus, "the author and perfecter of faith, who for the joy set before Him endured the cross…" (v.2 NASB). Is it possible to endure, with joy, the crosses in life? If the answer is "no," then the issue may be one of purpose.

---

5   Ibid.

This is why the early church counted unpleasant circumstances a joy and privilege, even in persecution. They had a reason for existing, and it was not grounded in personal popularity and acceptance. They were driven by a mission, the mission of Jesus in their lives. If that is true in your life, it will infuse you with delight no matter the situation.

Go deeper by joining us in prayer for Day 8.
Visit www.strategicrenewal.com/21days

DAY 9

> The chief end of man is to glorify God
> and to enjoy Him forever.
>
> *Westminster Catechism*

Most of us have seen some version of Scrooge in the story *A Christmas Carol*. The most significant event in this memorable story was the transformation of Mr. Scrooge's perspective on life. After investing his days in greed and self-centered living, he received a vision of how his life might end. He saw himself kneeling before his own neglected grave and was jolted by the realization that there are far more important things in life than the petty focus that had always consumed him. From that moment on, Ebenezer Scrooge devoted his energies toward a new mission in life. What changed him? He realized that he was living for the wrong reason. When he came to terms with the possible outcome of his lifelong course, his whole purpose for living changed. So can yours.

Living In His Steps

The Bible consistently reaffirms that Jesus came with a clear sense of purpose. All of the works, miracles, and deeds of Jesus ultimately flowed from His mission of being born to die in order that we might live. His mission was to shed His blood on the cross that you and I might receive the forgiveness of sins and that He might give eternal life through Himself. He came to give you a reason for existing here on earth and He wants you to know why you are here. Following in Christ's steps brings new meaning to the hours you're investing in that job, hobby or volunteer commitment.

Eternal, Earthly, and Explicit Purposes

Three aspects of purpose are important as we seek to renew our minds in truth and live a deeper existence. They are eternal, earthly and explicit. *Eternal purpose* is the overarching reason for our existence, not just in this life, but for eternity. Why do you exist? Isaiah 43:7 says, "Everyone who is called by My name, whom I have created for My glory; I have formed him, yes, I have made him." Here, as in other biblical texts, we are reminded that we are created by Him and for Him.

Our *earthly purpose* helps us to identify why we are here on earth—right here, right now. This is the "why" behind our brief journey on this earth. Can you specifically and passionately articulate your mission on earth? You have one for sure. You do not need to "develop" it as God already has made you to fulfill it. You need to discover it, live it deeply and complete it.

Even more specific expressions are called *explicit purposes.* These bring meaning to the varying roles in our lives. For instance, you can clarify and write your specific purpose in your roles as a parent, an employee, a volunteer at church, etc. What is your purpose in these roles and responsibilities? If you don't know, then it's really important to take time to think about it.

So, What Will You Do?

I've heard and told the story of the three bricklayers many times. You've probably heard it too but the relevance is obvious as we wrap up this chapter.

Once there were three bricklayers. A passerby asked each one of them what he was doing. The first man answered gruffly, "I'm laying bricks." The second man replied, "I'm putting up a wall." The third man said enthusiastically, "I'm building a great cathedral where people can encounter God, families can find refuge and society can be served."

A deeper life embraces the noble purposes of God for everyday life. We are not just fulfilling mundane tasks. We are not simply working on temporary projects. We are joining the God of the universe in a plan that matters for eternity. "Why am I here?" is an essential question for strategic daily renewal and the experience of winning over the devil, flesh and the world around us. God has a place for everyone, and everyone can find their place. Now, go build that cathedral.

Go deeper by joining us in prayer for Day 9.
Visit www.strategicrenewal.com/21days

DAY 10

Everyone who is called by My name, whom I have created for My glory; I have formed him, yes, I have made him.

Isaiah 43:7

A wise man once said, "Great minds have purposes. Others have wishes." Are you spending your life wishing and wondering, or do you have a God-given purpose that compels you? Once you are able to capture the vital essence of your *eternal, earthly,* and *explicit* purposes, you will no longer be discouraged with days that feel meaningless.

Your Eternal Purpose:

The Westminster Catechism states that the "The chief end of man is to glorify God, and enjoy Him forever." This reflects the purpose behind our very existence now and in eternity. In the space below, write out your own statement about God's eternal purpose for your life. (It may be the same as the Westminster statement or slightly modified to reflect your unique thoughts):

Your Earthly Purpose:

What thoughts do you have about your unique purpose on this earth, as a specific expression of your theology and identity? Consider what you would like to be chiseled on your tombstone and write a summary paragraph:

Your Explicit Purposes:

Using the chart on the following page, list the key roles and relationships you fulfill in life. In the adjoining space, begin to craft a purpose statement for each function.

Why am I Here? Part 3 **51**

Role:	Purpose:
Example: *Mother*	My purpose as a mother is to teach my children to love God. Therefore, I will seek to raise them with no regrets, modeling and instructing them in godliness and putting their interests above my own.
Role:	**Purpose:**

When your days feel meaningless, your direction is fogged, and your head is filled with the disturbing dictates of the world around you—your purposes can prevail. Think about them, pray about them, speak about them and live in light of them every day.

> Go deeper by joining us in prayer for Day 10.
> Visit www.strategicrenewal.com/21days

DAY 11

What Really Matters?

> And also if anyone competes as an athlete, he does not win the prize unless he competes according to the rules.
>
> *II Timothy 2:5*

Growing up, one of my favorite games was Monopoly. I have fond memories of Friday nights at my older brother's home, embroiled in a fierce competition to put one another out of business through our dominant real estate holdings. I am not sure that I ever actually read the official rules for Monopoly. I just adapted to the rules my brother taught me.

As I've played Monopoly over the years with other friends and acquaintances, I've realized that many of us have made up our own rules about how and when to collect money, when you can and cannot start trading properties, and how you can manipulate things when you are about to go bust. When people play the same game using different rules, conflict and confusion ensue.

In life, many of us are playing by rules we learned somewhere and from someone along the way. We embrace our rules, which may or may not be based on reliable truth. We soon realize that other people have their own sets of rules. Not only can we become confused on how the game of life is to be executed, but conflict abounds as our values clash with those of others. Of course, Monopoly is just a game of little consequence. Life, on the other hand, is a contest that requires clarity and conviction about the principles that make for satisfaction and significance.

Our Set of Working Values

What if someone were to come up and ask, "Can you explain your values in two minutes or less?" Could you identify some uncompromising principles that are real for you and woven into the fabric of your daily existence? Are they so clear and dominant in your thinking that they are a framework for your daily life? Do you have a certain awareness that these principles spring from the Word of God?

I believe every one of us has a longing to embrace wisdom in such a specific way that it results in a system of principles that will guide and guard our daily journey. We need a set of personal convictions which we will not compromise. This can be described as a value system.

Paul reminds us in 2 Timothy 2:5, "If anyone competes as an athlete, he does not win the prize unless he competes according to the rules." Values matter. A clear understanding of the unchanging rules of the game matters.

The Value of Integrity in Values

Tony Campolo has described an insightful social research poll conducted on fifty people, all over the age of ninety-five. They were asked, "What would you do differently if you had life to live over again?" The top three answers were these: I would reflect more, risk more, and do more things that would live on after I'm dead.[6]

A Christian interpretation of this would be, "I would take more time to clarify the principles that really matter. Then, after ex-

---
6 "If I had it to Live Over Again," https://soundcloud.com/tonycampolo/if-i-had-it-to-live-over-again.

amining their eternal value, I would take the risk and boldly live out my life based on these principles." This is the collective voice of fifty people with ninety-five years of experience. Still, a person doesn't have to reach this age to learn these lessons.

Those who live meaningful lives are people of deep conviction. To develop conviction you must slow down and ask yourself what matters. Then, check and see if there is a disparity between what you say and what you do. In the beginning, it may have to be a daily process. With consistent practice, though, the principles will become clear both in your words and life. Your life of integrity.

> Go deeper by joining us in prayer for Day 11.
> Visit www.strategicrenewal.com/21days

DAY 12

> They profess to know God,
> but in works they deny Him….
>
> *Titus 1:16*

When it comes to values I see two important factors. One is what I call our declared values; the other involves our demonstrated values. Declared values are what we say. Demonstrated values give evidence to what really matters by how we live. To avoid the dilemma of double-minded living and practical hypocrisy, we must come to a point where these two factors align.

This idea can be stated as an equation:

Declared + Demonstrated = Integrity

Declared – Demonstrated = Hypocrisy

The task for us, if we are to live an integrated, meaningful life, is to come to a place of clarity and regular application so that our declared and demonstrated values are consistent and complimentary, not contradictory. A shallow, occasional engagement with the vital issue of values will not create a satisfying life. We must go deeper.

Making it Practical

Shortly after I became a father, I felt an urgency to pass on to my children a set of practical ideals they would remember after they grew up and left our home. This aspiration forced me to give my first serious consideration to the task of clarifying values. The result was not profound or pithy, but it helped my children remember some "rules for the game of life."

I was not sure how to do this, but over time, I drafted a simple set of "12 Principles" that I clarified and communicated to them in creative ways over the years. Each principle took the form of a little slogan. Over time, I memorized these principles and, for the most part, so did the kids. Back in the day, I gave each of them a three-ring binder, professionally printed, with the full text of the verses. These have become real treasures to them. Today, as adults (and now with their own children) we talk often of our "Twelve Principles." I have a feeling they will be passed on for generations to come. I have also organized my personal values, using the acrostic from my first name. This makes it easy to remember. I try to review it every day, think about it regularly and am still adding scriptures and detailed applications to each principle.

Clarifying Your Values

Formulating your DECLARED values:

Write brief description in the space below of the convictions you determine to be most important in your life. These are principles that you hope you would never compromise in the course of daily living.

Discovering your DEMONSTRATED values:

Here are some steps to assess your demonstrated values before you actually finalize the process by writing your values down:

- What dominates my thoughts? What do I really spend most of my time thinking about?
- Where do I spend my time? Time is life. If our time is spent on things that do not reflect our declared values, we have dissonance.
- How do I spend my money? Where your treasure is, there will your heart be also.
- How do I react? What do my reactions reveal about the values that motivate me?
- What would a brutally honest friend or associate say? Imagine their answers. Or, if you are really ready for some "reality," ask them. What demonstrated values do they see in your life that may be negative, destructive, or contradictory in comparison to your declared values?

In a spirit of humble dependence on God, review your *DECLARED VALUES* (in the first part of this exercise) and compare them to your *DEMONSTRATED VALUES* (in the second part) then seek His grace to deal with any contradictions you discover.

Organize to Memorize

Having thought deeply about your guiding principles, it may be worthwhile to organize them in an easy-to-remember form. Use this as a time to reaffirm your declared values that are supported by your demonstrated values and trust God for power to live accordingly.

Go deeper by joining us in prayer for Day 12.
Visit www.strategicrenewal.com/21days

Day 13

What Shall I Do?

*A life in which anything goes will ultimately
be a life in which nothing goes.*

John Maxwell

Years ago, a newspaper headline told about three hundred whales that died after becoming marooned in a shallow bay. They became trapped while pursuing sardines. One commentator observed, "The small fish lured the giants to their death. They came to their violent demise by chasing small ends, by prostituting vast powers for insignificant goals."[7]

Like these giant mammals, the vast power of God's Spirit in the lives of believers is often prostituted when we chase things that are ultimately insignificant. If only we would think and do things that are ultimately important.

The Power of Clear Priorities

The practical crucible of life teaches us that we cannot do everything and we certainly cannot please everyone. The nature of society's increasing array of choices pulls us in many directions at once. The needs of people around us compel us to respond to more

---
7   William Cook, Success, Motivation, and the Scriptures (Nashville: Broadman, 1974), 127.

expectations than we can possibly bear. That is why we need clear priorities.

I define priorities as the commitments we put first in our lives because we believe they are important. The key term here is "commitments." This resolve is distinguished from the act of "prioritizing," which is a simple function of time management and ordering daily tasks. Instead, we are addressing the basic areas of one's life-focus – the commitments to which we dedicate large portions of our energy. These commitments ultimately determine our goals and the way we spend our time.

In *The Deeper Life* book, SIX GUIDEPOSTS are described to help define our commitments. In summary, they are:

Scripture – Because truth is the basis of our commitments

Stewardship – Because we are accountable to God for our commitments

Servanthood – Because we are called to love others through our commitments

Significance – Because not all commitments have equal eternal value

Satisfaction – Because we enjoy good reward in keeping vital commitments

Stability – Because our commitments provide essential boundaries and balance

Urgent vs. Important

Former President Eisenhower has been credited with saying, "The urgent is seldom important, and the important is seldom urgent." This was brought home years ago in a tragic way when the now defunct Eastern Airlines flight 401 crashed between New York and Miami. As the crew prepared to land, they noticed that a light, which indicated the landing gear was down, had failed to respond. They weren't sure if the problem was the light or the landing gear. The flight engineer attempted to remove the bulb, but it wouldn't loosen. Other members of the crew tried to help him. As they struggled with the bulb, no one noticed that the plane was losing altitude. It crashed into a swamp and people died. This experienced crew of highly trained technicians and pilots became preoccupied with an inexpensive light bulb and a plane full of passengers became tragic casualties.[8]

All of us are on a lifelong journey. If we don't take time to prepare our hearts and thoughts according to an integrated foundation of truth, we will constantly be displacing things that matter with the inexpensive light bulbs that surprise us with their urgent screech every day of life.

> Go deeper by joining us in prayer for Day 13.
> Visit www.strategicrenewal.com/21days

---

8   Cited by John Maxwell in Developing the Leader Within You, (Nashville: Thomas Nelson, 1993), 28.

DAY 14

If you put first things first, the second things will get thrown in.
But if you put second things first,
then you lose both first and second.

C.S. Lewis

One of my mentors early in my ministry often reminded me, "the power of 'no' is in a stronger 'yes.' If we have not clearly embraced the 'yes' commitments of solid priorities, we will be subjected to unimportant, urgent and unplanned influence affecting our fruitfulness for Christ and relationships with others.

This is like the old lighthouse keeper who worked on a rocky stretch of coastline. Every month he would receive a new supply of oil to keep the light burning. Because he was near the shore, he had frequent guests. One night, a woman came from a nearby village and begged for some oil to keep her family warm. Another time, a father asked for some to use in his lamp.

Someone else needed oil to lubricate a wheel. All of these requests sounded legitimate, so the lighthouse keeper granted the requests. Toward the end of the month, he noticed that his supply of oil was very low. Soon it was gone, and the beacon went out. That night, several ships were wrecked and lives were lost. When the authorities investigated, the man was very repentant. Yet, through all his excuses and pleading, the investigators told him, "You were given oil for one purpose: to keep the light burning."[9] This was their conviction. It had failed to be his.

God has given us a theology, an identity, and a purpose for a reason: They help us identify the priorities that matter to Him. We need to strengthen our conviction to live for Him, even when other people may not understand our "no." Jesus said, "Seek first His kingdom and His righteousness; and all these things shall be added to you" (Matthew 6:33). Now here is a life-management method that really brings some lasting results.

Articulating Your Priories

Use the chart to write down your specific and most important commitments you will seek to pursue and protect on a daily basis. These are the yeses that will help you fulfill the Effective Purpose Statements you wrote out on Day 10. (See example below)

	Role *Mother*	Role *Wife*	Role *Small Group Leader*
Priority 1	Make prayer a priority in our home	Serve in ministry with my husband	Pray for the needs in our group

---

9 Cited by Maxwell in *Developing the Leader Within You*, 25–26.

	<u>Role</u>	<u>Role</u>	<u>Role</u>
Priority 1			
Priority 2			
Priority 3			
Priority 4			

Go deeper by joining us in prayer for Day 14.
Visit www.strategicrenewal.com/21days

DAY 15

How Shall I Do It?

> I press on toward the goal to win the prize
> for which God has called me heavenward in Christ Jesus.
>
> *Philippians 3:14*

Rising up the side of a mountain in Zacapa, Guatemala, is a staircase containing 250 steps. It is located on the campus of Hope of Life, a ministry dedicated to serving the poor throughout the country. The steps were constructed in order to assist the staff in getting quickly from one area of the campus to another. On the day the steps were completed, ministry founder Carlos Vargas, held a contest for any staff members willing to race up the steps. Cash prizes were promised to the three runners who could reach the top first.

Among the 10 contestants willing to race was a sixty-year-old man weighing 200 pounds. The remaining runners were between the ages of 15 and 20. Although all the runners took off at the starting pistol, the group soon spread out as some fell behind. The sixty-year-old was among the leaders throughout the race. After finishing in second place, the old runner immediately lost consciousness. He received oxygen and water, and then was asked why he risked his life to win against the young boys. The dedicated man answered, "I ran because I needed to win the prize. I have a daughter and she is going to die unless she has an operation. I need that prize money to pay for her surgery."[10]

Paul described how we must fight, work, and strain with purpose, direction, and discipline. In Philippians 3, he focused on running and finishing the race in order to win the prize that God promised him, the high call of Jesus Christ. In New Testament times, chariot races were held in many cities of the Roman Empire. Paul may have pictured himself as a charioteer as he described a decisive moment of the race, when he strained forward to what lay ahead. Intensely pressing toward the goal of the prize at a high speed, Paul noted that even one glance backward could be tragic and, perhaps, even fatal in this race. He realized that Christians must forget what they've achieved in the past and must, with newly bestowed grace, strain forward with all their might.

In these races, judges would sit by the goal, carefully prepared to render their final decision. In Paul's letter to Timothy, he wrote "There is laid up for me the crown of righteousness, which the Lord, the righteous judge, will award me in that day; and not only to me, but also to all who have loved His appearing" (2 Timothy 4:8). This kind of race and reward demands our all.

An Explanation of Goals

The word *goal* originally meant "pole, rod, or stick." Historically, *goal* has meant something visible that would be positioned at the end of a racecourse so that all participants could keep their eyes on the rod or pole. When this word is used, it signifies a point that has been set as a boundary or finishing point.

In Greek, the word is *scopos*, from which we get the word "scope." It represents a mark on which someone would fix his or her

---

[10] Vargas, Carlos, *Dreams are Cheap* (Guatemala, Punto Creativo, 2013), 85.

eyes. From these two definitions I've developed this working model: A goal is a mark toward which you direct your life so that you can accomplish your priority commitments and live with integrity.

After we clarify our priorities and come to valid conclusions about what really matters, we take the next step of establishing specific marks, or targets. It's these marks that we set our eyes on, in an all-out effort to see our priorities become reality.

When it comes to goals, we must continually give our hearts to God and discard meaningless and temporal ambitions. We must submit our plans to the Lord to confirm that our goals are the same as His.

> Go deeper by joining us in prayer for Day 15.
> Visit www.strategicrenewal.com/21days

Day 16

> The world stands aside to let anyone pass
> who knows where he is going.
> *David Staff Gordon*

> Commit to the Lord whatever you do,
> And he will establish your plans.
> *Proverbs 16:3*

We often miss the mark when it comes to what our goals should be. We can get wrapped up in tangible, temporal things and lose sight of the biblical perspective of goals. With a clear and practical ***theology*** shaping our ***identity*** and motivating our ***purposes***, we have a strong foundation and framework. Knowing our ***values*** and the best ***priorities*** to pursue sets us up for specific action. Now it's time to consecrate our hearts and minds to the Lord in order set some ***goals***.

Consecrated Plans

Use this guide to help develop goals that will accomplish the priorities you identified in the previous chapter.

My Priority:

(Write the priority these goals will accomplish)

Goals (Rough Draft):

Write the goals you will need to aim toward in order to achieve this priority. This is a rough draft so don't scrutinize too much at this point.

1.

2.

3.

Step One: Consecration

What areas of my life will I have to surrender to God in order to accomplish these goals? (Review Proverbs 16:1–4)

Step Two: Preparation

Are these goals specific? If not, write the specifics which ought to be clarified?

Are these goals measurable? How will you know if your pace is on target for accomplishing these goals?

Are these goals attainable? If not, adjust the ambition of the goal. If the hindrances can be overcome, how?

Step Three: Imagination

In what way will these goals require faith?

What positive outcomes will occur if you achieve these goals? Write these down.

What promises of God's word will you focus on to keep your faith growing? Write them down.

When and how will I systematically pray about these targets?

Step Four: Execution

Now write a final version of your goals, having completed the first three steps.

Step Five: Evaluation

(Complete this step once a month)

Are these goals still integrated and consistent with the foundations of theology, identity, purpose, values, and priorities? If not, how can you make adjustments?

Am I on target with the established measurements? If not, how can I make adjustments to stay on course?

How am I regularly trusting God by faith for these goals?

Step Six: Celebration

(To be completed just before the goals are met)

How will I celebrate the accomplishment of these goals? When will this occur? Who will I include?

How can I give praise and thanksgiving to God for this achievement?

> Go deeper by joining us in prayer for Day 16.
> Visit www.strategicrenewal.com/21days

DAY 17

When Shall I Do It?

*If I could, I would stand on a busy corner, hat in hand,
and beg people to throw me all their hours.*

Bernard Berenson

Just what is this thing called time? You can ask many different people and receive a variety of answers. I define time as my habitual expenditure of the stewardship of life. Time is a "stewardship" because our lives are not our own.

We tend to segment our understanding of time with labels like *work time, family time, leisure time, nap time, meal time,* and the like. In reality, it is all *God's time.* Since it is His, we'd better be careful in what we do with it.

Elisabeth Elliot expressed this same conviction when she said, "Time is a *creature*—a created thing—and a gift. We cannot make any more of it. We can only receive it and be faithful stewards in the use of it."[11] God has entrusted every person with life; time is life and life is time.

Our History with Time

Frustration with time began early in man's history. History re-

---
11 Elliot, Elisabeth, *Discipline, The Glad Surrender* (Grand Rapids, MI: Baker Publishing Group, 1982)

cords a statement of a man named Plautus who, in 200 B.C., cursed a sundial. He uttered, "The gods confound the man who first found out how to distinguish hours... who in this place set up a sundial to cut and hack my day so wretchedly into small portions."[12]

Have you ever felt that way about time? Fifty years ago futurists were peering into their crystal balls and predicting that one of the biggest problems for coming generations would be decisions concerning their abundance of spare time. Authorities testified before a senate subcommittee in 1967 that by 1985 people could be working twenty-two hours a week or twenty-seven weeks a year, and could retire at age thirty-eight. Five decades have passed since then. Maybe I missed something.

"Paradoxical as it may seem," says one commentator, "modern technological and industrial society, in spite of an incredible proliferation of labor-saving and time-saving devices, has not given people more time to devote to their all-important task of spiritual things. In fact, it has made it exceedingly difficult for anyone except the most determined to find any time whatever for these tasks." It is his opinion that "The amount of genuine leisure available in a society is generally in inverse proportion to the amount of labor-saving technology it employs."[13] In a nutshell, the more sophisticated we become, the less time we have.

Perhaps you have read the well known piece of prose that reads, "I have only just a minute, only sixty seconds in it, forced upon me, can't refuse it, but it's up to me to use it. I must suffer if I lose it, give account if I abuse it, just a tiny little minute, but eternity is in it."

This connection between time and eternity urges us to be sure we understand time from God's perspective. God's Word gives us a solid understanding of the biblical concept of time. Paul wrote,

---

[12] Quoted by Daniel J. Boorstein in *The Discoverers* (New York: Random House, 1983), 25.
[13] Shumacheer, E.F., *Good Work*, (New York: Harper & Row, 1979), 25.

"Be careful how you walk, not as unwise men, but as wise, making the most of your time, because the days are evil. So then do not be foolish, but understand what the will of the Lord is." (Ephesians 5:15–17)

Today is the day to begin a biblical, habitual expenditure of the stewardship of life through strategic daily renewal. Through a deeper approach, you can "win" the battle for the effective use of time.

> Go deeper by joining us in prayer for Day 17.
> Visit www.strategicrenewal.com/21days

DAY 18

> We must work the works of Him who sent Me
> as long as it is day; night is coming when no one can work.
>
> *John 9:4*

On November 19, 1863, a consecration service was held on a blood-covered battlefield at Gettysburg, Pennsylvania. Just that month 51,000 soldiers were killed, wounded, or missing in that decisive battle, so a national cemetery was being proposed for this site.

The original keynote speaker for this solemn ceremony was a man named Edward Everett. He was an extraordinary orator with cultured words, patriotic fervor, and public popularity. As a former governor and congressman, this sixty-nine-year-old statesman was a natural choice for this momentous gathering. Through an unanticipated turn of events, the commissioners of this service also invited President Abraham Lincoln. When the commissioners learned that the president planned to attend, they asked him to offer "a few appropriate remarks" as well.

When the day came, Edward Everett rose to give his speech according to plan. His memorized oratory flowed with masterful fluctuation and dramatic gestures. Everyone, including President Lincoln, was captured with his eloquence. Finally, an hour and fifty-seven minutes later, Everett concluded with the crowd applauding enthusiastically.

A short while later, President Lincoln was introduced. His notes consisted of two simple handwritten pages, with thoughts borne out of his own great burden and tears over the wartime situation of the country he led and loved. With very little gesturing, but deep personal passion, he delivered his own Gettysburg Address. In two minutes he was finished.[14]

Almost one hundred and forty years have passed since that day of solemn remembrance. No one can recall one line from the two-hour speech of the orator. Yet, Lincoln's two minutes of passion—flowing from deep conviction and clear purpose—are among the most memorable thoughts in the history of our nation. This illustrates the difference between minutes and moments.

Chronos vs. Kairos

Let's pause for a moment to define two Greek words that translate into time. The first is *chronos*, from which we get the word "chronology." This is the idea of continuous time that is measured in hours, minutes, or seconds. This is the clock that pushes us to the next appointment and runs out before we have finished with our daily responsibilities.

The second word for time is *kairos*, which is the idea of a fixed moment or season of opportunity. This is the period of the day when something special and truly memorable happens. This is the experience of our life when time stands still and something truly "timeless" happens.

Chronos is quantitative. Kairos is qualitative. The difference between these two words is the difference between a minute and a moment. A minute is measured by seconds, or by a clock. The experience and opportunity measure a moment.

---
14 Swindoll, Charles, *The Quest for Character,* (Portland: Multnomah Press, 1987), 119–124.

Most of our planning, when it comes to time, deals with the "minutes" of life instead of the "moments." However, biblical emphasis is almost opposite. Yet this does not mean we should neglect structure and organization. After all, "God is not the author of confusion" (1 Corinthians 14:33). What it does show is that we have not understood the value of time until we firmly grasp, actively anticipate, and purposefully pursue the moments God places before us. We can learn to "seize the moments," not just "spend the minutes."

One of the most important elements in *kairos* living is remembering to be open to the people who enter into your daily life. Are you ready and willing to make an eternal impact on them or is your day so tightly scheduled that God-given purpose is forgotten? Wise time-management includes being open to the spontaneous work of the Holy Spirit. In short, make the most of your time.

Go deeper by joining us in prayer for Day 18.
Visit www.strategicrenewal.com/21days

Day 19

How Will I Finish?

*The great use of one's life is to spend it on something
that will outlast it. For the value of life is computed,
not by its duration but by it donation.*

William James

When you woke up this morning, it is possible you started your day believing a lie. The deception is subtle, even subconscious. The falsehood is seldom articulated or analyzed. What is this fallacious fib? The essence of the untruth is that it does not matter how you lived your life, why you lived your life or even that you lived your life.

The circulating lie is that only a select and special minority make a significant impact on this world. But if legacy was primarily about money, only the rich really matter. If legacy were about achievement, only the driven and extraordinarily skilled would count. If legacy were about knowledge, only those with superior IQ's would be respected.

The truth is everyone has the potential of leaving a legacy in this life. This chapter will help you understand why—and how.

We Need Your Legacy

The world around you needs your legacy. The story and significance of your life is waiting to be told to a world hungry for meaning and models. The drama, defeats, determination and dialogue of your journey offers meaning to eager hearts—around the world and right under your nose.

What Is a Legacy?

Legacy is defined as something transmitted by or received from another who has preceded us in this life. But this simple description hardly captures the essence of this eighth and ultimately important question.

In the end, a deeper life must be a life deposited into the fertile soil of eternal souls through the transforming seeds of truth. A legacy is an eternally significant investment of one's life in the lives of others. Legacy allows each of us to "outlive our life" and leave behind a testimony of worship, integrity and non-conformity in this world.

I hope by now you have been deeply challenged to live with a rock solid, regularly reaffirmed foundation of knowing God, embracing your core identity and affirming God's purpose for your life. I pray that your desire to live by a clear set of values, embracing the best priorities and fulfilling those priorities through meaningful goals and effective use of time is being fulfilled. Yet, the end game of this process of daily renewal is that you leave a legacy for others to embrace and experience for their own good. As you make the time to clarify your answers to the foundational questions of this book you are not just penning words, or typing ideas, you are crafting an autobiography—to be read by those walking in your footsteps.

Benjamin Franklin said, "If you would not be forgotten as soon as you are dead, either write something worth reading or do something worth writing." This book, and your engagement with the process of strategic daily renewal, is intended to help you compose the insurance policy of an unforgettable life.

We've heard many times that it's not how you start the race but how you finish that matters. Legacy really is at the core of asking, "How will I finish?"

We cannot control when we will hit the finish line of life, but we can intentionally focus our energies on how we will cross that line.

> Go deeper by joining us in prayer for Day 19.
> Visit www.strategicrenewal.com/21days

DAY 20

> An inheritance is what we leave for others.
> A legacy is what we leave in them.
>
> *Daniel Henderson*

I hope you feel empowered with the assurance that you can truly live a life of lasting influence. Now, what can you do every day—for many days, to eventually shape a legacy that will be remembered long after you are gone? Consider these practical reminders.

The hard part about leaving a legacy is that it can only be fashioned over time and in the whirlwind of relentless spiritual battle. That's the nature of life. Because it is hard to navigate in a vortex, the daily commitment to this entire renewal process is vital.

I remember consulting with one of my mentors during a very difficult season of ministry. He listened, and then also shared some stories from a chapter of his own life, one that was also very painful. He offered practical wisdom I will never forget. "I decided that I could not waste my energies on things I could not control. I had to give my best efforts every day to what I COULD control." In his situation, he could not control the attitudes of other people, the reaction of his critics or the attendance figures of the church. He could control his own walk with God, his attitude, his exercise and diet routines, as well as his primary relationships.

Each of us must give relentless attention to the daily issues we can control. That is why our worship, integrity and non-conformity to the world are vital for building a legacy—a day at a time.

So, what can you leave as a visible reminder of your legacy? Consider writing two letters:

End of Life: Remembering that "an inheritance is what we leave for people and a legacy is what we leave in them" -take some time to write an "end of life" letter. Imagine it is the last hour of your life. Address the letter to the most important people of your journey. Describe what you hope you left "in" them. As you write, consider these themes: What do I want others to remember about me? What opportunities and risks have enriched my life? What has God's blessing looked like during my journey? What regrets must I surrender and trust to the mercy of God? Be as honest and specific as possible.

After you finish the letter, ask yourself: "What do I need to focus on every day in order for this letter to be an authentic representation of my legacy?"

First Minute in Heaven: Imagine you have just arrived in Heaven. Based on all you know from the Bible, imagine this new experience. Write a "first minute in heaven" letter. Address the letter to the Lord. What are you feeling about Him at this moment? What are you glad you did while you were on earth? What do you hope He will say to you and about you? What might you wish you had done on earth, before this moment in eternity?

After you finish the letter, ask yourself: "What do I need to focus on every day in order for this letter to be a letter of complete joy and ultimately honoring to my Lord?"

Well Done!

The ultimate goal of our legacy is the "Well done!" commendation of our Christ in eternity. The earthly benefit of our legacy is that we inspired those who knew us to embrace the same goal, walking along the path that has been made clear by the footprints we leave behind.

Go deeper by joining us in prayer for Day 20.
Visit www.strategicrenewal.com/21days

DAY 21

Conclusion

*The great thing is to be found at one's post as a child of God,
living each day as though it were our last, but
planning as though our world might last a hundred years.*

C.S. Lewis

Former US. Senate Chaplain Richard S. Halverson once shared a story about living a deeper, more intentional life –

"You're going to meet an old man someday down the road – ten, thirty, fifty years from now – waiting there for you. You'll be catching up with him.

What kind of old man are you going to meet? He may be a seasoned, soft, gracious fellow – a gentleman who has grown old gracefully, surrounded by hosts of friends, friends who call him blessed because of what his life has meant to them. Or he may be a bitter, disillusioned, dried-up old buzzard without a good word for anyone – soured, friendless, and alone.

That old man will be you. He'll be the composite of everything you do, say, and think – today and tomorrow. His mind will be set in a mold you have made by your beliefs. His heart will be turning out what you've been putting into it. Every little thought, every deed goes into this old man.

Every day in every way you are becoming more and more like yourself. Amazing but true. You're beginning to look more like yourself, think more like yourself, and talk more like yourself. You're becoming yourself more and more.

Live only in terms of what you're getting out of life, and the old man gets smaller, drier, harder, crabbier, more self-centered. Open your life to others, think in terms of what you can give, your contribution to life, and the old man grows larger, softer, kindlier, and greater."[15]

This same wisdom, applicable to both men and women, has been expressed before but in fewer words: "Do not be deceived, God is not mocked; for whatever a man sows, that he will also reap" (Galatians 6:7). As you come to the end of this devotional, the real journey begins.

When we think about the little old man or woman we hope to meet someday, we must realize that every choice, every day, matters – and shapes the person we are becoming.

My prayer for you, my friend, is the same as was Paul's hope for the Colossian believers. I pray you will be filled with the knowledge of God's will in all spiritual wisdom and understanding, so that you may walk in a manner worthy of the Lord, to please Him in all respects, bearing fruit in every good work and increasing in the knowledge of God.

As we continue one day at a time down the road of life, we have choices with every step. Choose well and you will meet a little old man or woman who will step across the finish line into eternity as a Christ-honoring overcomer. May God in His infinite patience

---

[15] Richard S. Halverson, quoted by Daryl Witmer, "As Time Goes On, You Become Your Choices," *Bangor Daily News,* February 3, 2007.

and grace bring forth the fruit of a deeper life in the days that are before you.

>Go deeper by joining us in prayer for Day 21.
>Visit www.strategicrenewal.com/21days

About the Authors

Daniel Henderson

For over three decades Daniel Henderson has been guiding individuals, leaders and churches to embrace experiences of powerful spiritual renewal. He has served as senior pastor to thousands in congregations in California and Minnesota. Today he speaks across the nation at leadership conferences and local churches while coaching pastors and business leaders in the principles of a strategic and spiritually significant life. He is a husband, father, grandfather and author of numerous books, including *The Deeper Life, Satisfying the 8 Vital Longings of Your Soul; Old Paths, New Power* and *Transforming Prayer: How Everything Changes when You Seek God's Face*. For more information about Daniel, visit strategicrenewal.com and 64fellowship.com.

Brenda Brown has been teaching on principles of purposeful living for over twenty-five years. She is co-author with Daniel Henderson of the book, *The Deeper Life, Satisfying the 8 Vital Longings of Your Soul* and author of an upcoming companion devotional for women. As a Life Coach, Brenda enjoys helping women discover their purpose and build a strategic plan to help navigate life's changing seasons. She is a wife, mother and grandmother. For more information on Deeper Life Coaching with Brenda, visit strategicrenewal.com.

Also leading in the interactive prayer experience:

Tony Brown

Prior to joining Strategic Renewal as Chief Operating Officer, Tony was best known for his expertise in logistics for well-known retail clothing companies. As a Christ follower and former global supply chain executive, Tony understands the struggles Christian business professionals face – how to live out their faith on the job, and how to balance family and work while actively serving in local church ministry. Tony is a husband, father and grandfather, and now enjoys working with Daniel Henderson and Strategic Renewal – *Helping Pastors Succeed, God's Way.*